How To

SAVE THE
PLANET

How To

SAVE THE
PLANET

By BARBARA TAYLOR

Illustrated by
Scoular Anderson

FRANKLIN WATTS
A Division of Scholastic Inc.
New York Toronto London Auckland Sydney
Mexico City New Delhi Hong Kong
Danbury, Connecticut

For Carissa, to help her save the planet

First published 2001 by Oxford University Press
Great Clarendon Street, Oxford OX2 6DP

First American edition 2001 by Franklin Watts
A Division of Scholastic Inc.
90 Sherman Turnpike
Danbury, CT 06816

Catalog details are available from the Library of Congress
Cataloging-in-Publication Data

ISBN 0-531-14640-5 (lib. bdg.)   0-531-14821-1 (pbk.)

Printed in China

Contents

WHY THE EARTH NEEDS SAVING

When astronauts first set foot on the moon, one of the most exciting things their photos showed was something most people thought they already knew about: Earth. When viewed from space, it seems almost impossible that a tiny speck of rock could be home to such a fantastic variety of plants and animals—as well as more than six billion people.

Viewed from space, it also becomes clear that the Earth is an island—it's out there on its own, and we all depend on it for survival.

So why does the Earth need saving? Well, to put it bluntly, because of us! Today, the world population stands at over six billion. By the end of the twenty-first century, it could reach eight or ten billion. To satisfy the needs of these growing numbers of people, human beings are slowly but surely destroying the planet. We're using up the planet's natural resources; polluting the land, seas, and skies; choking the air with fumes; and clearing forests and other precious wildlife habitats to make way for more buildings. The way we live is damaging the very thing that gave us life in the first place: planet Earth.

I think we're in a no-win situation here!

This book tells you everything you need to know about the different problems facing the planet. After reading it, you'll know all about

❀ how the Earth's atmosphere protects the planet

❀ holes in the ozone layer, and how they affect Earth and us

7

- ✿ why the Earth is getting warmer
- ✿ what pollutes the air and water
- ✿ what causes acid rain
- ✿ how we can save energy
- ✿ why cars and planes are bad news
- ✿ how waste can be recycled
- ✿ why it's important to save wild places such as rain forests

You'll also find special sections that tell you what you can do to help save the planet. Because everything in the world is interconnected, you'll find that a lot of the suggestions overlap. For instance, recycling paper cuts down on the piles of waste that pollute the Earth, but it also saves forests, because fewer trees have to be cut down to make new paper.

I'm helping save the planet

CHAPTER ONE

HOLES IN THE SKY

Imagine it's a skin-blistering, eyeball-burning summer day, and you're escaping from the heat under an umbrella. Then someone comes along and silently cuts holes in the umbrella. Ouch! Two hours later, you're sunburned, sore, and angry.

This is pretty much what's happening to the Earth. The Earth has its own built-in sunscreen, made of a layer of ozone that stops many of the sun's ultraviolet rays from getting through the atmosphere.

9

These rays can cause all sorts of problems, from skin cancer to eye diseases—and not only in humans. They are also bad for some plants, making them grow smaller leaves and suffer more from pests and diseases. Too many ultraviolet rays damage or kill off the microscopic sea creatures that feed fish, seabirds, and the great whales. Holes in the ozone layer are pretty scary because they could eventually threaten all life on Earth.

What Is the Ozone Layer? ....

Ozone is an invisible gas that is actually a form of oxygen, the gas we need to breathe. Ozone has three oxygen atoms per molecule instead of the usual two. It is found high up in the atmosphere. The ozone layer is about 9 to 55 miles (15 to 90 kilometers) above the surface of the Earth. Without it, the sun would burn us to a crisp.

The reason the ozone layer is so fragile is that there is very little of it. The total amount of ozone between Earth and space consists of a layer only .1 inch (3 millimeters) thick. The layer is spread unevenly in a band of the atmosphere, so it's a lot thicker in some areas. Most ozone is produced over the tropics, where the sun's rays are strongest and most direct. This is because ozone can only be made with the help of the sun's ultraviolet rays.

What's Making the Holes? ....

Several chemicals, which are released into the atmosphere by people, are causing holes in the ozone layer. Here's a list of the main culprits:

* In the past, chlorofluorocarbons (CFCs), which were used in aerosols, refrigerators, and air conditioners, destroyed a lot of ozone. They are now banned. Old machines containing CFCs have these chemicals removed before they are discarded.

I'm just going to remove your CFCs— it won't hurt a bit!

❀ Hydrochlorofluorocarbons (HCFCs) are replacing CFCs in some products. They only have about 10 percent of the ozone-destroying power of CFCs, but they still do some damage.

❀ Methyl bromide is a pesticide used by some farmers, especially those growing fruit and flowers. By 2005, it will no longer be used in the United States.

When these chemicals reach the ozone layer, ultraviolet rays break them down, releasing chlorine or bromine atoms. These atoms join up with oxygen atoms from ozone molecules and destroy the ozone.

One molecule of chlorine can destroy 100,000 molecules of ozone. As the ozone layer is weakened and thinned, it lets through more ultraviolet radiation, which speeds up the destruction of the ozone layer even further.

Where Are the Holes? ....

In the 1980s, scientists were shocked to discover that the amount of ozone over Antarctica had decreased by more than two-thirds. The development of ozone holes over Antarctica happens for a few months each year. The long Antarctic winters produce frozen clouds high in the atmosphere, where ozone-destroying reactions occur.

As well as these temporary holes, the Earth's entire ozone layer seems to be thinning. In 2000, scientists found that almost two-thirds of the ozone layer over parts of northern Europe was gone for a few days.

The United Nations Environment Program has estimated that a permanent 10 percent reduction in the ozone around the globe will cause an extra 300,000 cases of skin cancer and 1.6 million cases of eye cataracts each year.

Repairing the Ozone Layer ....

Governments around the world have agreed to stop using CFCs and cut back on the use of other chemicals that damage the ozone layer. But there are still other problems.

Many of the alternatives to CFCs, such as HCFCs, still contain some chlorine. And although there are some completely ozone-friendly alternatives, such as butane and propane, not everyone is using them. Many of the CFC alternatives have also been found to contribute to global warming and are already being phased out in some countries.

Even if all ozone-destroying substances were banned tomorrow, the CFCs already in the atmosphere will still hang around for twenty years or more, poking holes in the ozone layer.

Rich and Poor ....

In developing countries, such as China and India, more people are buying things like refrigerators and air conditioners. The types they buy contain lots of CFCs. Governments in industrialized countries should do as much as they can to help developing countries use ozone-friendly alternatives.

Go for Green ....

There is a lot being done to tackle this issue already. But there are still some things you can do to help save the ozone layer:

 When your family or someone you know is buying a new refrigerator or freezer, make sure they ask for an ozone-friendly one. Also get them to check that the CFCs in the old refrigerator are going to be drained out and recycled. Never just dump an old one. CFCs are only released when refrigerators are made or thrown away, not when they are being used.

 Check the labels on stain removers, shoe cleaners, dyes, glues, and correction fluids, and try to avoid ones with ozone-destroyers in them. The ingredient to look out for is methylchloroform (1. 1. 1-trichlorethan).

Don't forget to use hats, sunglasses, and sunblock to protect your skin from the sun's ultraviolet rays.

CHAPTER TWO

A WARMER WORLD

Have you noticed that winters are getting warmer?
That you've been getting along with only three
thermal vests when you once needed four?

Ever wondered why the planet seems to be heating
up? Well, it's no secret—it's called global warming.

What Is Global Warming?

Many scientists are convinced that the world is getting
warmer because of human actions. We are releasing
too many harmful gases into the Earth's atmosphere.
These gases trap some of the heat given off by the
Earth so that it can't escape into space. It's as if the
Earth is trapped inside a huge greenhouse.

17

Greenhouse gases are produced by car exhaust; the burning of coal, oil, and gas in power stations and factories; and rotting waste. They also come from CFC-containing refrigerators, air-conditioning units, and styrofoam. (CFCs are twenty thousand times better at trapping the Earth's heat than the most common greenhouse gas, carbon dioxide.) Most climate-changing pollution comes from industrialized countries, such as the United States, Canada, Japan, Australia, and European nations. Power stations and cars in these countries pump out vast amounts of carbon dioxide and other greenhouse gases.

So What? ....

Well, at first it might sound like good news that the Earth is getting warmer. Some scientists predict that the temperature could go up by as much as 39°F (4°C) by the end of the twenty-first century.

Those of you living in chilly countries probably think it would be nice if the weather warmed up a bit. But it's not as simple as that. A 39-degree increase in temperature would make the world hotter than it has ever been in human history. This would create major problems all over the world:

❀ There will be bigger floods in coastal areas as the water in the oceans expands and glaciers and ice sheets melt even more than they already do.

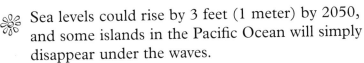

❀ Sea levels could rise by 3 feet (1 meter) by 2050, and some islands in the Pacific Ocean will simply disappear under the waves.

❀ Areas once important for growing food, such as the Midwestern United States and the Ukraine, might become too dry for agriculture. Local food shortages, especially in Africa, could lead to higher food prices and more famine.

❀ The patterns of rainfall and winds could change, making the weather more unpredictable. This would also cause a lot more violent weather, such as typhoons, hurricanes, tornadoes, and storms.

❀ Warm ocean currents such as the Gulf Stream could change direction, making some countries colder instead of warmer.

❀ The changing climate conditions would make it difficult for some plants and animals to survive.

Be an Earth Scientist
HELP REDUCE
GREENHOUSE GASES

WHAT YOU'LL NEED

- a young tree (choose a variety that grows naturally in your community)
- a shovel
- a stake
- string or something to tie the tree to the stake
- compost
- mulch (chips of bark or other plant materials)

WHAT TO DO

1. In autumn or spring, dig a deep hole in a place away from buildings where a tree will have plenty of space to grow. (Get permission from an adult first!) Some trees grow very tall, and their roots spread out farther than you think.
2. Put some compost in the bottom of the hole.
3. If the tree is over 5 feet (1.5 m) tall, put a stake in the hole. (This will protect the tree from wind.)
4. Loosen the tree roots carefully and place the tree in the hole. (Make sure you plant the tree right-side up!)

5. Fill the hole with soil. Stomp the soil down with your feet.
6. Soak the ground around the tree with about two buckets of water to encourage the roots to grow.
7. Sprinkle mulch onto the surface to hold the moisture and stop weeds from growing.
8. Keep the tree watered as it grows.

WHAT HAPPENS?

Trees (and other plants) soak up carbon dioxide and use it to make their food and build new plant material. As it grows, your tree will help reduce the amount of one of the greenhouse gases in the atmosphere, thus reducing global warming.

The Story of the Earth's Changing Climate

Since the Earth formed some 4.6 billion years ago, the climate has been constantly changing. At times it was a lot warmer than it is now. At other times it was a lot colder, with much of the land covered in ice. These very cold times are called ice ages. The causes of changes to the Earth's climate include

- continents drifting around the globe
- changes in the speed and direction of warm and cold water currents in the oceans
- changes in the amount of radiation given off by the sun
- changes in the path of the Earth's orbit around the sun, which changes the amount of sunlight falling on different parts of the Earth
- dust from space, meteorites hitting the Earth, or volcanoes on Earth blocking out the sun and cooling down the climate. This is one explanation for why the dinosaurs died out, along with more than half the species of plants and animals living 65 million years ago.

Hey, who turned out the lights?

Climate Change Today ....

One of the problems about climate change today is that it's difficult, even with the latest supercomputers, to predict how the climate of a whole planet will change in the future.

There are so many things to take into account, such as how fast the oceans will warm up and how much heat clouds will reflect and absorb. The only thing scientists are fairly sure about is that global warming is happening now, and we really should do something about it.

What Can Be Done? ....

Global warming is such a big problem that it needs big solutions. Countries need to get together and

24

agree on what to do. Their governments can make changes, such as

* cutting down on greenhouses gases and using sources of energy such as wind, wave, or sun power, which don't produce these gases

* removing carbon dioxide gas from power stations before it is released into the atmosphere

* burying carbon dioxide underground or in the oceans

* preventing the burning of the rain forests, which releases greenhouse gases into the atmosphere

* improving public transportation so that people use cars less often

* encouraging people to insulate their homes to stop heat from escaping

Go for Green

Here are some things you can do to help slow down global warming:

 Use less electricity and gas so that power stations will pump less carbon dioxide into the atmosphere. Switch off lights and lower heat when rooms are not being used, and use low-energy light bulbs.

 Use cars less. Take public transportation, ride your bike, or walk if you can. This will keep you in shape, too!

 Help plant trees, which will soak up carbon dioxide.

26

CHAPTER THREE

AIR POLLUTION AND ACID RAIN

In Victorian times, large cities in Britain, such as London, Birmingham, and Manchester, were covered by thick, yellow fog in the winter. These fogs were caused by smoke from coal fires in homes and factories, which built up in the still, cold air. The fogs were called "pea-soupers" because they were thick and murky, like pea soup.

I wish they'd change the menu. I'm getting bored with pea soup every day.

Little was done to control the problem until December 1952, when a horrible fog settled over London. Traffic ground to a halt, twelve thousand people died, and many people became seriously ill.

27

Still, it took another four years before the Clean Air Act of 1956 was passed by the government. The act contained laws to control the amount of smoke produced by factories and homes. Many towns and cities were made into smoke-free zones.

The Air We Breathe ....

We've already seen how gases from cars, factories, and power stations can cause global warming. There is also the added problem of the air pollution they cause. A lot of this is from invisible gases such as carbon monoxide, sulfur dioxide, nitrogen oxides, and ozone. You're probably breathing in some of these right now!

Traffic fumes and other forms of air pollution can make illnesses like asthma much worse. However, asthma has been around since long before cars were invented. The ancient Egyptians used to treat it with crocodile dung.

CHECK LOCAL
POLLUTION LEVELS

One way to tell how polluted the air is in your area is to carry out a lichen survey. Lichens are strange living things that usually look like flat green or orange pizza crusts stuck to stones or tree bark. Sometimes they look like beards. Lichens are made of a fungus and an alga living together.

Lichens are very sensitive to air pollution. If you can't find any, your air is badly polluted.

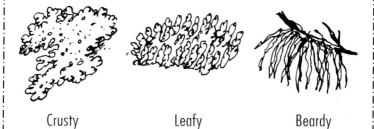

Crusty   Leafy   Beardy

Crusty lichens will endure some pollution.
Leafy lichens will only stand a little bit of pollution.
Beardlike lichens will only grow in clean air.

Killer Rain ....

Air pollution isn't just a problem in the air. It also mixes with water vapor in the atmosphere to make acid rain. All rain is naturally slightly acidic, but gases from power stations and vehicle exhaust make it much more so. These strong acids eat away at the stone of buildings and statues and make them crumble away. Acid rain also damages trees and weakens them by changing the chemistry of the soil around their roots. This means the trees are less able to cope with disease, insect attacks, and other problems. Trees with needle-like leaves are affected the most.

About 50 percent of the trees in Germany, Britain, and the Netherlands have damage that might have been caused by acid rain. There is some dispute over whether damage is caused directly (to the needles) or indirectly (by affecting resistance to disease).

Rivers and lakes are also affected by acid rain. One-quarter of the lakes in the Northeastern United States are damaged. In Sweden, thousands of lakes have virtually no fish at all.

Be an Earth Scientist
CHECK ACID LEVELS IN
YOUR RAIN

WHAT YOU'LL NEED

- a red cabbage
- a saucepan
- a colander
- a jug
- 3 jars
- vinegar
- baking soda
- rainwater

WHAT TO DO

1. Chop up a few red cabbage leaves and put them in a saucepan with 2 cups (.5 liter) of tap water.
2. Ask an adult to help you boil the leaves for ten minutes.
3. Let the mixture cool, then pour it through the colander into the jug to get rid of the pieces of cabbage.
4. Pour a small amount of the cabbage water into each of the three jars.
5. Add a few drops of vinegar to one jar, a teaspoon of baking soda to the second jar, and some rainwater to the third jar.

WHAT HAPPENS?

Acids, such as vinegar, will turn the cabbage water pink. If your rainwater is very acidic, it will turn the cabbage water to a strong pink color. Baking soda is a base (the opposite of an acid) and will turn the cabbage water green. (This is a great experiment, but don't try drinking the results!)

I said fruit tea, not vegetable tea!

31

Air Action ....

Governments can take action to reduce the amount of air pollution in a number of ways. They can require factories and power stations to use more efficient boilers and furnaces that produce less pollution. Also, fuels such as coal and oil can be processed so that they produce less pollution when they burn. For instance, fitting flue gas desulphurization (FGD) to power stations reduces the amount of sulfur dioxide (SO_2) they pump into the atmosphere.

Adding lime to soils, lakes, and rivers is one way of making them less acidic. This is very expensive, however, and scientists don't completely understand how this changes the chemistry of the water or soil.

Catalytic converters (CATs) in cars reduce the amount of pollution in their fumes. Cars that use fuel more efficiently create less air pollution in the first place.

Go for Green ....

Here are some things you can do to lessen air pollution and the effects of acid rain:

 Use less energy, especially electricity for lighting, heating, and exercise machines. This will mean less pollution from power stations.

Bike to school or arrange a "walking bus," where you meet up with other children and all walk to school safely together.

 Keep a regular check on the lichens in your area to be sure air pollution isn't getting worse.

 Buy second-hand toys or do some swaps with friends. Factories would make fewer new things, and less pollution would be pumped into the air.

CHAPTER FOUR

WATER POLLUTION

Where would we be without water? Well, nowhere actually. Without water there would be no life on this planet. Water covers almost three-quarters of the Earth's surface.

You'd think that with so much water around, it would be hard to do much damage to the oceans and seas. Yet all too often, the oceans are used as giant dumping grounds for oil, sewage, toxic chemicals, and radioactive waste. Nowadays, we are pumping in so much pollution that some seas, such as the Baltic, the North, and the Mediterranean, can't dilute the poisons quickly enough. Many beaches have become too polluted for safe swimming.

A Threat to Life

In 1989, pollution from rivers such as the Po in Italy created huge mounds of slimy green algae in the Adriatic Sea between Italy and Yugoslavia. Sewage pollution encourages algae to grow in large numbers, using up all the oxygen and killing fish and other water life.

The freshwater in rivers, lakes, and underground water is also threatened by the poisons leaking from garbage dumps, chemicals from industry, and pollutants from farms, such as pesticides and fertilizers that are washed into the water.

Oops!
Oil Spills at Sea

You know how much of a mess it makes if you accidentally drop a glass of juice? Well, oil spills are much worse! Since 1975, enough crude oil has been spilled to fill almost twelve hundred Olympic-sized swimming pools.

They don't mean that literally, you know.

Here's a list of some notable oil spills:

- 1978: the *Amoco Cadiz* spilled 223,000 tons of oil off the coast of France.
- 1989: 38,000 tons of oil were spilled into Prince William Sound, Alaska, from the *Exxon Valdez*. Between 260,000 and 580,000 seabirds and hundreds of seals, bears, deer, mink, and river otters were killed. A total of 1,056 miles (1,700 km) of shoreline was affected by the oil.
- 1993: the *Braer* spilled over 85,000 tons of oil off the Scottish coastline.
- 1996: the *Sea Empress* lost about 73,000 tons of oil in Pembrokeshire, South Wales.
- 1999: the *Erika* sank in a gale off the coast of Brittany, France, releasing at least 15,000 tons of oil and killing more than 58,000 seabirds.

Oil tanker accidents are responsible for only a small percentage of the oil polluting the world's oceans. Much more of the oil released by ships comes from tankers cleaning out their tanks. Other ways that oil gets into the sea include oil and gas exploration and drilling at sea, oil refineries on land, and people carelessly getting rid of engine oil.

Be an Earth Scientist
PROVE THAT OIL DAMAGES FEATHERS

WHAT YOU'LL NEED
- bicycle oil
- a feather
- paper towels
- cotton balls
- dishwashing liquid

➤

WHAT TO DO

1. Lay the feather on some paper towels and put a few drops of water on the feather. Look carefully at the shape of the water drops.
2. Dry the feather and put a few drops of bicycle oil on it. Spread the oil over the feather with a cotton ball and then drop some water on top. What shape are the water drops now?
3. Put some dishwashing liquid and water into a bowl and wash the oiled feather. Is it easy to get the oil off?

WHAT HAPPENS?

The clean feather is waterproof, so water forms round drops and rolls off the surface. On the oily feather, the water soaks in. Oily feathers stick together and cannot keep out cold and moisture. When birds try to clean their oily feathers, they swallow the poisonous oil. Even with soapy water, it's not easy to clean feathers. Some oiled seabirds can be cleaned up after an oil spill, but many are covered in too much oil to be saved.

Pulling the Plug ....

Have you ever wondered what happens to your bath water when you pull out the plug? Or where all the waste goes when you've flushed the toilet?

Dirty water usually goes to a sewage treatment plant to be broken down and cleaned up before the water is put back into rivers or the sea.

Special bacteria can be used to eat up the sewage and destroy harmful dirt and germs. But often the waste does not get enough treatment and pollutes rivers or the sea. Many communities do not have sewage treatment plants at all.

Sewage poisons wildlife. It uses up oxygen as it breaks down, leaving less for the wildlife in the water. It also contains millions of bacteria and tiny creatures that cause infections and diseases.

Be an Earth Scientist
MAKE YOUR OWN
WATER FILTER

WHAT YOU'LL NEED

- a large plastic bottle
- a large plastic cup
- scissors
- cotton balls
- gravel
- sand
- filter paper

WHAT TO DO

1. Make a mixture of muddy water.
2. Cut the bottom off a large plastic bottle and wedge a piece of cotton in the neck of the bottle.
3. Turn the bottle upside down and fix it firmly in the plastic cup.
4. On top of the cotton, add a layer of stones and gravel and a layer of fine sand.
5. Put a piece of filter paper on top of the sand.
6. Pour the muddy water carefully through the filter.

➤

Dirty Water, Clean Water ....

The amount of nasty stuff that gets dumped into our rivers, lakes, and seas by big companies, farmers, and individuals needs to be reduced or cleaned up so that it doesn't pollute the water.

Better sewage treatment could make a difference, too. But it's not always easy to find out who has caused the pollution or to make people obey water pollution laws. And improving sewage treatment plants costs money.

41

Go for Green

Here are some things you can do to help save the world's water:

 Save water by taking a shower instead of a bath and turning off the tap while you are brushing your teeth.

 Don't use more bubble bath or shampoo than you need to. Their chemicals pollute the water and make it harder to clean.

 Put a water container in the garden to catch rainwater for the plants instead of watering them with tap water.

 Don't pour oil or paint down the drain. Ask an adult to take them to a local dump to be recycled.

 Encourage adults not to use pesticides in the garden, so that they won't get washed into the water underground.

 Don't dump litter in the sea, on beaches, or in rivers.

 Report any water pollution you see to your town council or to the water company.

CHAPTER FIVE

ENERGY

We need energy for everything we do—running, jumping, walking, talking, and sleeping. Even the laziest couch potatoes need some energy to reach for the remote control or lift another potato chip to their mouths!

Why do they waste all that energy chasing a small round object they never even eat?

We get the energy we need from the food we eat. We burn the food inside our bodies to release energy.

From the earliest days of human history, people have used other sources of energy, such as wood to burn on fires.

Nowadays, people in industrialized countries (such as Europe and North America) use vast amounts of extra energy to heat and light their homes and run washing machines, vacuum cleaners, televisions, computers, cars, and other machines. North America has only 4 percent of the world's population but uses 25 percent of the world's energy. India, on the other hand, has 17 percent of the world's population but uses only 2 percent of the world's energy.

Where Does Energy Come From? ....

Our main source of energy is the sun. Every half hour, the Earth receives more energy from the sun than the total energy released by all the coal, oil, and gas burned in the world for a year.

Plants use the sun's energy to make food. Animals get their energy by eating plants or other animals. Over millions of years, the dead remains of plants and animals have turned into coal, oil, and gas.

These are called fossil fuels because they were formed from the fossilized (preserved) remains of plants and animals.

When we burn fossil fuels in power stations or in our homes, we release the sun's energy stored in animals and plants that lived long ago. Unfortunately, we also add to the problems of global warming and acid rain.

Energy on the Run ....

The trouble with fossil fuels is that once they are used up, that's it. We can't get them back. And we're going through them at frightening speed. If we continue to use fossil fuels at the same rate as we do now, this is roughly how long they will last:

- coal: 200–1,500 years

- oil: 40–60 years

- natural gas: 60 years

Coal provides about 40 percent of the world's energy today and is one of the main fuels used in power stations to make electricity. Natural gas provides about one-fifth of the world's energy.

Oil supplies about half of the energy we use. If all the barrels of oil produced in a day were laid end to end, the line would stretch twice around the equator.

Nuclear Power ....

Some power stations use nuclear power (energy from splitting atoms) to make electricity. Nuclear power stations don't produce greenhouse gases or cause acid rain. But they do have a couple of major drawbacks.

Accident at Chernobyl

Chernobyl, Ukraine, 1986

The accident at the Chernobyl nuclear power station in 1986 was far worse than any oil spill. An explosion in the nuclear reactor immediately killed thirty-two people and caused several injuries and additional deaths. Thousands of people in the area are still suffering from the aftereffects of the disaster.

Clouds of radiation from the explosion spread over Europe and Scandinavia. Huge numbers of plants and animals were poisoned. Even reindeer in northern Scandinavia and sheep in Britain were killed as a result of eating lichen that had been poisoned by the radioactivity.

➤

CHERNOBYL

The risk of dangerous accidents at nuclear power stations is one reason that many people are against producing electricity this way. Another reason is that nuclear power stations produce very dangerous radioactive waste. This gives off radiation so deadly that it must be kept out of harm's way for hundreds, possibly thousands, of years. At present there is no safe way of doing this.

Renewable Energy ....

There are alternate ways of making electricity from energy sources that are cleaner, safer, and won't run out:

❀ solar power, which uses the power of the sun

❀ wind turbines and windmills, which harness the energy of the wind

❀ water power, using the power of falling water

- 🌼 wave power, which traps the energy of the waves

- 🌼 tidal power, which harnesses the energy of the tide as it comes in and goes out

- 🌼 heat from underground rocks (geothermal power), used to make electricity

- 🌼 biogas, a fuel source made from animal dung and human sewage

49

These alternative energy sources are better for the environment in many ways, but they still have their problems. Wind turbines, windmills, and solar power stations take up a lot of land; setting up tidal power stations can destroy wildlife habitats; and harnessing geothermal power means drilling into rock, destroying land and causing pollution. Also, energy from alternative sources can be expensive and unreliable.

Be an Earth Scientist
MAKE A SOLAR PANEL

WHAT YOU'LL NEED
- a black plastic trash bag
- a shallow cardboard box
- tape
- scissors
- clear plastic tubing about .3 inch (8 mm) in diameter
- modeling clay
- thin wire
- wire cutters

WHAT TO DO
1. Line the box with the black plastic bag, holding it in place with tape.
2. Cut a piece of plastic tubing about three times the length of the box.
3. Place the tubing inside the box in an S shape. Use small lengths of wire, poked through the sides of the box, to hold it in place.
4. Seal one end of the tube with modeling clay and fill the tube with cold water. Make sure the unsealed end of the tube is pointing upward when you add the water. ➤

5. Leave your solar panel in the sun for a few hours and then pour the water out into a bowl.

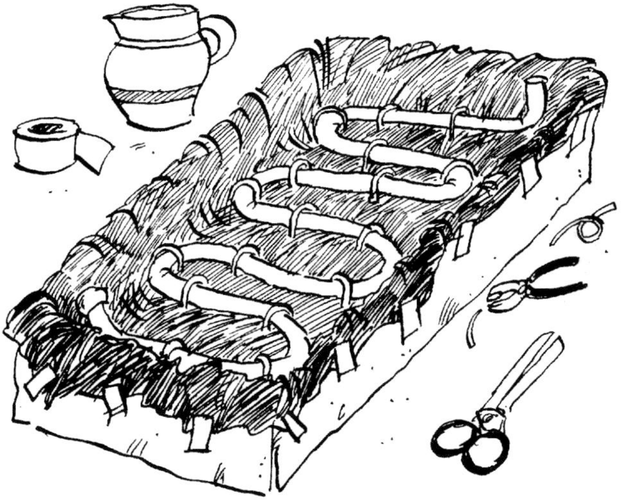

WHAT HAPPENS?

The energy from the sun heats up the water in the tube just like a real solar panel. The black plastic absorbs the sun's heat and helps warm up the water.

The Wind-Up Radio

Radios are usually powered by batteries or plugged into electrical outlets. It takes energy to make batteries. When they are thrown away, the metals leak out and cause pollution. An inventor named Trevor Baylis has invented a radio that doesn't need electricity or batteries. You just wind the radio up for about 20 seconds, and it plays for about an hour.

As well as saving energy, the wind-up radio can be used by people who do not have an electricity supply and can't afford batteries.

Energy for the Future ....

To keep our use of energy from causing so many problems, such as global warming and acid rain, governments could put more money into renewable forms of energy, such as solar, water, or wind power.

The best way to reduce our energy problems, however, would be to use less energy in the first place. Governments could encourage people to insulate their homes, fit a jacket around the hot water tank, and have their windows double-glazed so that heat energy stays inside the home and doesn't escape.

Go for Green

Here are some things you can do to save energy:

 If you're cold, put a sweater on; don't turn the heat up. If you're hot, turn the heat down rather than opening windows while the heat is still on.

 Persuade your parents to buy low-energy lightbulbs. Some energy-efficient lightbulbs use 80 percent less energy than ordinary ones and last eight times longer. So energy-efficient bulbs help the environment and save money!

 Dry clothes outdoors instead of using a drier.

When boiling a kettle, only put in the amount of water you actually need, and use it right away.

Use your hands instead of energy-guzzling machines. Wash dishes instead of using a dishwasher, and brush your teeth with an ordinary (not electric) toothbrush.

CHAPTER SIX

TRANSPORTATION

Today, there are hundreds of different types of transportation to move people and goods around, from bicycles and roller blades to cars, buses, trucks, airplanes, and even space shuttles. If all the cars in the world were parked end to end, they would stretch around the equator more than thirty-six times.

Traveling in Time

Until about 250 years ago, the main forms of transportation were feet (walking!), ships, and animals (horses, donkeys, and camels). But in the eighteenth, nineteenth, and twentieth centuries, a whole bunch of inventions changed the face of transportation forever.

- Early 1700s: Horses pulled railway coaches along tracks.
- 1783: The first hot-air balloon took off.
- Early 1800s: Steamboats and trains were developed.
- 1863: The world's first underground train system was built in London, England.
- 1880s: The first cars went on sale to the public in Europe, and the first electric trains were tried out.
- 1900–1910: The first airplanes were developed.
- 1904: The first mass-produced car, the Ford Model T, was invented in the United States.

That's not what I meant by a model T!

- 1935: The first highway was built, in Germany.
- 1961: First space flight.
- 1990s: Very large cargo ships transported goods over the oceans. Each ship used enough power to light half a million light bulbs.

The Trouble with Transportation ....

Most forms of transportation have a bad effect on the environment.

Something bothering you?

Making cars, trains, ships, and planes uses up energy and materials. Then there's all the land that has to be cleared to make way for roads and railways.

Cars, trucks, and trains guzzle up energy in the form of fuel as they zoom along. The fumes they pump out pollute the air and harm living things.

Ships pollute the sea and use up energy. Airplanes use enormous amounts of fuel—the more weight they carry, the more fuel they use.

CATs in the Car ....

Today, many new cars are fitted with a device called a catalytic converter (or CAT for short), which removes most of the harmful gases. The CAT fits inside the exhaust system of the car and only works with unleaded gasoline.

Sounds good, doesn't it? There's a snag, however. CATs do not remove carbon dioxide, so car fumes still contribute to global warming. Also, CATs are made of rare metals, and digging these metals out of the ground damages the environment. Yet another problem is that the CAT doesn't begin to work until the engine has warmed up, so on a short trip, it probably doesn't work at all.

Future Cars

Scientists are looking for new kinds of car fuel that will not pollute the environment. One day cars might be able to run on solar power—using the sun's energy to power car batteries. At the moment these cars are just experiments, but who can say what the future will bring?

Another source of fuel might be hydrogen taken from water. On the Earth, there is an awful lot of water from which hydrogen can be made. When hydrogen burns, the exhaust consists of steam, not polluting gases.

Cars powered by electric batteries are another possibility. Batteries aren't powerful enough for long journeys, however, and the power to recharge them has to come from somewhere. If the power comes from a polluting power station, then the cars will still be damaging the environment. Batteries are toxic when they are thrown away.

Cars can run on fuels such as ethanol or methanol, made from plants such as sugarcane.

Fuels made this way would be sustainable, because more plants could be grown to replace the ones used up. But large areas of the Earth would have to be taken up growing these plants, which might not be good news for the environment.

Top Transportation Tips ....

Governments can do a lot to encourage people not to use their cars so much. If public transportation were cheaper, more reliable, and more comfortable, people would use it more. Sixty cars, each carrying one person, use about sixteen times more energy than one bus carrying sixty people.

Governments could also do the following:

 encourage individuals and businesses to use trains more, especially for long-distance travel and carrying goods

❀ make bicycling safer by setting up bike lanes in every town and city

❀ stop companies from building out-of-town shopping centers, because most people have to drive to them

❀ build new houses near city centers and places where there are jobs, so that people don't have to travel so far to get to work

❀ make driving cars more expensive by raising the price of gas and parking garages. The money made from these extra charges could be spent on public transportation.

❀ only allow cars in city centers at certain times of the day

Go for Green

Here are some things you can do to cut down on the problems transportation causes:

 If you're planning a vacation or other long trip, get your family to go by train. It's better for the environment and can be more fun, too.

 Get your school or town to provide safe places to leave bikes, so that more people can cycle to school.

 If your family or friend plans to buy a new car, encourage them to get one with a catalytic converter (CAT).

 Buy local! Use local stores and buy food that is grown locally to cut down on the trips needed to transport people and goods.

 If the car you are in is stuck in a traffic jam for a long time, ask the driver to switch off the engine.

CHAPTER SEVEN

THAT'S GARBAGE!

Every month, each of us throws away our own body weight in garbage. That's not only leftover chips, old soda cans, and moldy fruit, but also newspapers, plastic packaging, old toothpaste tubes, clothes and shoes that are too small or out of date, batteries that have run out, broken electrical goods, old toys... the list is endless.

It says here just two days' issues of this newspaper would stretch higher than the top of Mount Everest!

I don't believe it.

Somebody who likes playing around with numbers has figured out that every American will leave behind a mountain of waste that is roughly four thousand times their body weight by the time they die. For Europeans, the figure is about one thousand times their body weight. For someone from Madagascar, the amount is only one hundred times their body weight.

63

The solution to the waste mountain is not for us all to move to Madagascar. We need to stop throwing things away and find ways to reuse them, fix them, or give them to someone who can use them. What would be better still is if we all stopped buying so many things in the first place!

What's Wrong with New Things? ....

Making new things uses up resources. Materials such as metal and oil (most plastics are made from oil) have to be dug out of the ground. This leaves nasty gashes in the landscape and destroys and pollutes wild places. What's more, these kinds of materials cannot be replaced once they have been used up.

Transporting raw materials to factories uses energy. The factories that make the goods use up energy too, usually from fossil fuels, which adds to the problems of global warming and climate change.

Then the goods are wrapped in a lot of unnecessary packaging (more waste) and transported to the shops (more pollution) to be used and thrown away on the garbage mountain.

Sure, it's nice to have new things, but we could make much better use of the things we have. Even small changes can make a big difference.

Think about this interesting little fact: if each of ten million office workers used just one less staple a day by reusing a paper clip, an incredible 120 tons of steel would be saved each year.

OFFICE MEMO
USE FEWER
PAPER CLIPS

Dead Bodies and Dung ....

The natural garbage produced by plants and animals (dead leaves, rotting wood, animal bodies, animal dung) is never wasted. Lots of living things, especially bacteria and fungi, find waste really yummy. Dead leaves make tasty snacks for worms.

As waste-gobblers eat, they break down the waste so that it can be used to build new living things and help them stay alive.

But natural garbage buried in garbage dumps can produce a gas called methane. This gas can make dumps explode. It also causes global warming.

WHUMP

In the Netherlands, 90 percent of the natural garbage from people's homes is recycled; in Denmark, 55 percent is recycled; and in Austria, the figure is 50 percent. Other countries could follow these good examples.

Be an Earth Scientist
RECYCLE YOUR GARBAGE: MAKE A COMPOST HEAP

If you have a garden, you can turn your old food waste and grass clippings into free fertilizer that helps plants grow.

➤

WHAT YOU'LL NEED

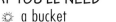

- a bucket
- fruit and vegetable peelings
- lawn clippings and leaves
- rabbit, guinea pig, or hamster droppings
- weeds

WHAT TO DO

1. Collect your waste in the bucket and pile it up in the corner of the yard. (You could ask an adult to help you make a compost bin from wood and chicken wire to stop the garbage from spreading over the yard.)

2. Keep the compost heap moist (but not wet) and make sure it is loose enough for air to circulate, so that living things can survive there.
3. You can cover the heap with a piece of old carpet or wood to keep it warmer so that it will turn into fertilizer more quickly.

WHAT HAPPENS?

Bacteria, fungi, and creatures such as worms, millipedes, slugs, and earwigs feed on the heap and make it rot into rich compost. All this feeding makes the heap heat up—within a week it might even be steaming!

➤

Compost takes up to six months to form, so don't expect things to happen overnight. Then you can mix it into the flowerbeds or the vegetable garden to make the soil rich. This is much better than buying bags of peat, which may have been dug up from peat bogs (important habitats for rare plants and animals).

Worm Power

If you don't have a yard, or enough room to make a compost heap, you can still make compost using a worm bin and some special compost worms called brandling worms. You can get the worms from someone else's compost heap or in fishing shops. Use the compost for your potted plants or give it away.

Wrap It Up

About a third of the garbage we throw out is packaging. Packaging is important—it keeps food fresh, makes freezing food possible, stops things from getting squashed or broken, and gives us information.

Your breakfast cereal would be pretty difficult to carry back from the supermarket without its box. And baked beans without the cans just aren't worth thinking about.

But a lot of the packaging we end up bringing home isn't really necessary. It just makes products look bigger and better than they really are. Easter eggs are a good example of this.

One of the most common types of packaging is the plastic bags we use to carry things home from stores. The handles cut into your hands like knives, and the bags often split open halfway home.

You're much better off with a basket, box, or canvas bag.

Once Is Not Enough ....

Getting rid of garbage by dumping it in holes in the ground or burning it in incinerators causes huge problems and harms the environment. The obvious answer is to recycle more of our garbage. This saves raw materials, cuts down on the energy we use, and reduces pollution.

You'd be surprised at what can be recycled. Hopefully, you already recycle your old newspapers, cans, and bottles. You can do all sorts of things with them if you use your imagination.

There are also places and organizations that recycle greeting cards (including Christmas cards), eyeglasses, video games, batteries, books, clothes, shoes, computer software, toner for photocopiers, print cartridges for computer printers, and many other things.

Paper

You probably know that paper is made from trees. But did you know that every year, each one of us uses up two trees' worth of paper and cardboard? At that rate, it won't take long to use up all the world's forests, together with the wildlife and people who live there. And making new paper could involve using chlorine bleach, which pollutes rivers.

71

Be an Earth Scientist
MAKE RECYCLED PAPER

WHAT YOU'LL NEED

- ☀ scrap paper
- ☀ a bowl
- ☀ a hand mixer or potato masher
- ☀ 4 pieces of thin wood, to make a 6 x 10-inch rectangle
- ☀ hammer, nails, and thumbtacks
- ☀ fine curtain netting, wire gauze, or the backing used for tapestry weaving
- ☀ blotting paper
- ☀ a rolling pin
- ☀ an iron

WHAT TO DO

1. Tear up the scrap paper and leave it to soak in a bowl of hot water until it's really soft and mushy. (You can add colored paints, tinsel, wool, leaves, or even pencil sharpenings to make your recycled paper look more interesting.)

2. While the paper is soaking, make a sieve to strain the water from the mushy mixture. Ask an adult to help you nail the four pieces of wood together to make a frame, then cover it with the net, gauze, or mesh. Fix the cover in place with thumbtacks or nails.

➤

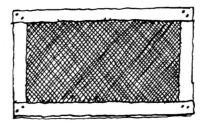

3. Put some blotting paper on top of several layers of newspaper.

4. Mash up the soaked scrap paper.

5. Dip the framed sieve carefully into the mashed-up mixture and hold it flat above the bowl to let the water drain through the sieve.

6. Turn the sieve quickly upside down and tip the layer of mushy paper onto the blotting paper.

7. Put another piece of blotting paper on top of the mushy paper and use a rolling pin to squeeze out as much water as possible.

8. Ask an adult to help you iron top layer of the blotting paper until the recycled paper is nearly dry.

9. Peel off the top piece of blotting paper and leave your recycled paper in a warm place to finish drying.

WHAT HAPPENS?

The fibers in the old paper spread out in the water. When you drain off the water, the wet fibers knit together to make a criss-cross network of fibers. This dries into sheets of recycled paper without any glue to hold the fibers together.

Cans

If all the cans thrown away in the United States every year were placed end to end, they would stretch beyond the moon. This terrible waste is completely unnecessary. All food and drink cans can be melted down and made into new cans. Making cans from recycled aluminum uses only 5 percent of the energy needed to make cans from raw aluminum. It is especially important to recycle aluminum cans because they take much more energy to make than steel cans do.

Glass

Glass is made mainly from sand and limestone—and there's hardly a shortage of those materials in the world. But digging sand and limestone out of the ground leaves great holes in the landscape and causes pollution. More important, making glass uses enormous amounts of energy. When a ton of recycled glass is used to make new glass, the equivalent of 36 gallons (135 liters) of oil is saved.

This is partly because recycled glass melts at lower temperatures than sand and limestone. Recycling also saves the energy needed to dig up the sand and limestone and deliver them to the glass factory.

If we throw our old bottles and jars away, they clog up garbage dumps and last forever, broken and buried in the soil. Recycling or reusing old glass bottles and jars changes all that.

Plastics

Plastics are a problem. Most plastics are made almost entirely from oil. Every year, as much oil is used up as it takes nature one million years to create. Plastics factories spew out polluting waste into rivers and sewers. One plastic, PVC, is a major source of dioxin pollution when it is burned. Dioxin is a chemical that is harmful to health, even in tiny amounts.

When most plastics are thrown out, they don't decompose (although some plastic bags are now designed to break down slowly). This means it's especially important to find ways of recycling and reusing plastics.

It's amazing what you can grow in old plastic yogurt cups.

Plastics are difficult to recycle, partly because there are so many different kinds. Mixed plastic waste can be recycled to make certain products, such as fence posts and traffic cones, but plastics need to be sorted and recycled separately to make high-quality products. It would be easier to recycle plastics if the industry set up more sorting facilities. It would also help if each product were made of one type of plastic, and if plastic products were clearly labeled so that people could easily sort them.

Dairies in the United States, Canada, and Sweden use plastic milk bottles that can be reused up to one hundred times each. Perhaps in the future, more products could be packed in reusable bottles.

Go for Green ....

Here are some things you can do to cut down on the amount of stuff you throw away:

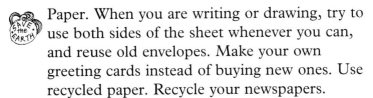

Paper. When you are writing or drawing, try to use both sides of the sheet whenever you can, and reuse old envelopes. Make your own greeting cards instead of buying new ones. Use recycled paper. Recycle your newspapers.

Cans. Take thermoses or reusable bottles on picnics or hikes. If your state has a deposit on cans, return them for money. If not, recycle cans at your local dump's recycling center.

Glass. Turn in your bottles for refunds, recycle them at your local dump, or reuse them.

Plastic. Buy glass containers instead of plastic ones when you can. Recycle old plastic containers, or reuse them as flower pots, for mixing paint, or for storing things. Avoid grocery bags, but if you have to get one, try to reuse it in some way.

SAVE WILDLIFE AND WILD PLACES

In this chapter we're going to look at the dangers facing the wildlife and wild places on this planet. First, try this true or false quiz to see how much you know and to find out some amazing facts.

True or False? ....

1. An area of rain forest the size of a soccer field is cut down every minute.

2. The Arctic is the only place on Earth that is not contaminated by poisonous chemicals.

3. Islands are especially at risk from habitat destruction. (Habitats are places where plants and animals live.)

4. The world's most endangered cat is the tiger.

79

5. Nearly half of crocodilians (crocodiles, alligators, caimans, and gharials) are endangered.

6. Dodos were killed off by global warming.

7. Rhinos are rare because people kill them for their tusks.

8. Orangutans will be extinct in the wild in five to ten years if rain forest destruction continues at its present rate.

9. Up to 80 percent of Britain was once covered in wild woodland; now only 1 or 2 percent is covered in trees.

10. Sharks are more likely to be attacked by people than the other way around.

Answers to True or False Quiz

1. False. An area of rain forest the size of six soccer fields is cut down every minute.

2. False. There is, alas, no place on Earth that is free from poisonous chemicals, not even the bottom of the oceans.

3. True. Islands are home to small numbers of unique wildlife that can be wiped out very quickly.

4. False. The Iberian lynx is the world's rarest cat. There are only a few hundred left, and they're teetering on the brink of extinction. Tigers are not doing very well either, though. There are probably only two to three thousand left.

5. True. They are threatened by loss of habitat, illegal hunting, competition with people catching the fish they eat, and egg collection.

6. False. Dodos became extinct because people hunted them, and rats and dogs ate their eggs.

7. False. Rhinos don't have tusks!

But rhinos are killed for their horns, which are made into dagger handles and used in traditional Chinese medicine.

8. True. There are now only about 5,500 orangutans left on Sumatra and 8,000–12,000 on Borneo, largely because the rain forests where they live are being cut down, and forest fires threaten them.

9. True. British woodlands have been cleared by people over the last four thousand years, and now Britain is one of the least wooded countries in Europe.

10. True. Only about twenty-four people are killed by sharks every year, but millions of sharks are hunted for their fins (for shark fin soup), meat, skin, and cartilage, while many more are killed accidentally in fishing nets.

Going, Going, Gone ....

Only a tiny fraction of all the life that has ever existed on the Earth has been preserved in some way—in amber, stuck in natural tar, deep-frozen in the soil, or trapped between layers of rock.

These remnants from the past tell us that the pattern of life is for new living things to develop, last for a few million years, and then die out, or become extinct. They are probably killed off by competition from other living things or changes in the Earth's climate.

Over the last four hundred years, living things have been dying out at a much faster rate than they usually do. One estimate is that the natural rate of extinction is one species every hundred years, while the speeded-up rate (caused by people) is one species every 15 minutes! At this rate, half of the planet's inhabitants could disappear during the next century.

Why Are Species Disappearing? ....

The main reason for the mass extinctions of recent years is the great increase in numbers of people—people who need somewhere to live, grow their crops, and keep their farm animals; people who build roads and take resources such as metals, trees, oil, and coal from the Earth.

Other threats to wildlife include

❀ people killing animals for their fur, skins, or other body parts (such as horns and tusks)

❀ pollution of the air and water caused by acid rain, pesticides, and increased ultraviolet radiation getting through the ozone layer

❀ global warming or climate change

❀ overcollection of animals for the pet trade or plants for gardens

- new species (such as cats and rats) being introduced to an area and destroying the wildlife already there

- diseases passed on from people to animals (gorillas have been badly affected by diseases such as measles and colds caught from people)

Does It Matter? ....

At this point, you might be wondering why we should bother to save all these wild places and the creatures that live in them. People have to live and eat, don't they? Well, yes, but it just so happens that we are not living in a vast empty space, but on a living, breathing planet. We are connected to all the living things around us through the food we eat, the air we breathe, the water we drink, and the soil we grow things in. Protecting the variety of life on Earth (biodiversity) helps keep the whole planet healthy and helps us survive at the same time.

On a selfish note, plants and animals that we have not even discovered yet could provide us with life-saving medicines and food in the future.

On an unselfish note, do we have the right to get rid of other living things, just because they don't suit our lifestyle? Don't they have as much right to live as we do?

Be an Earth Scientist
BUILD A POND

WHAT YOU'LL NEED

- ☀ permission to dig the pond
- ☀ a shovel
- ☀ some large stones or bricks
- ☀ plastic sheeting
- ☀ old cloth or carpeting
- ☀ old pond water or tap water
- ☀ soil
- ☀ pond weeds

WHAT TO DO

1. Choose a spot away from overhanging trees, so that the pond won't get clogged up with leaves in autumn.
2. Ask an adult to help you dig a hole about 7 feet (2 m) deep and 7 feet (2m) wide. The sides should rise in a series of shallow steps.

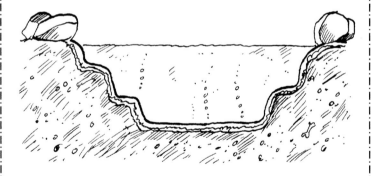

3. Clean out any sticks or stones from the bottom of the hole, put some old cloth or carpeting in the bottom, and line the hole with strong plastic.

➤

4. Hold the plastic in place with bricks or stones.
5. Cover the bottom of the pond with a layer of soil about 4 inches (10 cm) deep and fill it with old pond water or tap water to about 4 inches (10 cm) from the top (the level will go up when it rains).
6. Leave the water for a week and then add some pond plants on the ledges, together with some stones for animals to shelter under. Leave an area of sloping soil on at least one edge so that animals can get in and out of the pond.

WHAT HAPPENS?

Your pond should develop into a mini-ecosystem where you can watch changes in the web of life day by day. Garden ponds help frogs survive because so many natural ponds and ditches have been drained.

Note: If you cannot make an actual pond, an old sink or plastic bowl sunk in the soil or a tub of water on the patio will do instead.

Be an Earth Scientist
MAKE A BIRD FEEDER

WHAT YOU'LL NEED
- ☀ a piece of wood 12 x 16 inches (30 x 40 cm)
- ☀ four thin strips of wood to go along the sides
- ☀ glue
- ☀ a paintbrush
- ☀ wood preservative
- ☀ string or nylon thread

WHAT TO DO
1. Glue the four strips of wood along the edges of the large piece, leaving a gap in each corner for rain to drain out.
2. Paint the wood with a wood preservative that is not harmful to wildlife.
3. Ask an adult to help you drill two small holes at the base of each short side (see picture).
4. Thread string or nylon thread through the holes.
5. Hang your bird feeder from a branch or windowsill. (Keep it away from bushes where cats could leap out and attack the birds.)
6. Put food such as bread, nuts, and seeds on the feeder.

WHAT HAPPENS?
In cold weather, the food on your bird feeder could save lives. Once you start feeding the birds, do so regularly because they will come to rely on your food. In warm weather, there is plenty of natural food around, so there is less need to feed the birds as frequently.

Conservation Measures ....

Governments and companies control how land is
developed and can play a major part in preventing
habitat destruction. Industrialized countries have
destroyed much of their own wild places, yet they
often seem to be telling other countries not to do the
same thing. Developing countries need help, not
lectures. Many people think that the debts such
countries owe to industrialized countries should be
canceled in exchange for preserving their wild places.
Cutting back on pollution in all countries will also
help preserve habitats.

Governments could also

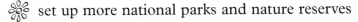 set up more national parks and nature reserves

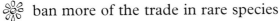 give people control of their own local
environment (such as forests) to encourage them
to protect their surroundings

ban more of the trade in rare species

catch poachers who try to capture rare species

breed rare species in zoos or botanical gardens
and reintroduce them into the wild

❀ plant trees that naturally grow in an area to replace those that are cut down

❀ pay for more research to identify new species and find out which ones are endangered

Go for Green ....

Here are some things you can do to save wildlife and wild places:

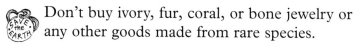 Don't buy ivory, fur, coral, or bone jewelry or any other goods made from rare species.

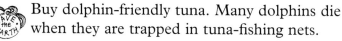 Buy dolphin-friendly tuna. Many dolphins die when they are trapped in tuna-fishing nets.

❀ Visit nature reserves and raise money for conservation organizations.

❀ Avoid disturbing plants and animals in the countryside, and don't pick or dig up wild plants.

❀ Make bird feeders and ponds to encourage wildlife in your garden.

❀ Don't use chemical pesticides in the garden, and use only organic fertilizers.

❀ Persuade your family not to buy furniture made of rain forest trees, such as mahogany or teak, unless it comes from a certified sustainable source.

CHAPTER NINE

HOW GREEN ARE YOU?

Now for the big test: let's see how green (earth-friendly) you are with this quiz. No cheating now!

1. Does your family use a drier instead of drying clothes outside?
2. Does your family intend to recycle the CFCs in their old fridge when they buy a new one?
3. Have you ever planted a tree?
4. If it is too hot in a room, you
    a) turn down the heat
    b) open a window
5. You get to school by
    a) walking, biking, or public transportation
    b) car
    c) sharing a car
6. Does your family car have a catalytic converter?
7. Do you turn off lights and heat in empty rooms?
8. Does your family use low-energy lightbulbs?

9. Do you leave the TV on all day?

I never turn the TV off.

10. Is your house insulated with double-glazed windows to stop heat energy from escaping?
11. You usually wash in
    a) the shower
    b) the bathtub
12. Do you leave the tap running when you brush your teeth?
13. Which of the following do you recycle?
    a) glass bottles   b) plastic bottles
    c) newspapers   d) cans
14. You
    a) use recycled paper
    b) reuse envelopes
15. Do you ever litter?
16. You use
    a) new shopping bags every trip to the store
    b) your old bags that you take shopping with you
17. Do you buy goods with as little packaging as possible?

18. Does your family buy organic products when it can?

19. You have, or have helped create,
   a) a pond
   b) a bird feeder
   c) a compost heap
   d) a wildflower patch

20. Do you support or raise money for "green" organizations (those that work to protect the planet)?

Scoring

1. yes 0, no 1
2. and 3. yes 1, no 0
4. a 1, b 0
5. a 2, b 0, c 1
6., 7., and 8. yes 1, no 0
9. yes 0, no 1
10. yes 1, no 0
11. a 1, b 0
12. yes 0, no 1
13. a 1, b 1, c 1, d 1
14. a 1, b 1
15. yes 0, no 1
16. a 0, b 1
17. yes 1, no 0
18. yes 1, no 0
19. a 1, b 1, c 1, d 1
20. yes 1, no 0

Green Rating

1–9 Oh, dear. You're about as green as an overripe strawberry, aren't you? Well, at least you've made a start by reading this book. Now that you know more about the problems facing planet Earth and how to solve them, maybe it's time to do your part to help!

10–18 Not bad. You're already doing a lot to save the planet, but you could do more. Maybe you just needed a few ideas to get you going on a greener lifestyle. Don't give up!

19–28 Wow, you're really doing your part to save the planet. Keep up the good work, and spread the word among your friends and family!

Can I Really Make a Difference?............

Saving the planet is an enormous task. The problems are huge and complicated, and a lot of the time even scientists don't fully understand what is happening. It's hard to predict what will happen to the Earth in the future. The amount of time people have lived on the Earth is like the blink of an eye compared with the long history of the Earth. Yet we have changed the face of the planet more than any other species that has ever lived here.

People have great power, and if enough people care about saving the planet, anything is possible. There is an old Chinese proverb that says, "The journey of a thousand miles begins with just a single step." Do you want to take the first step toward saving your planet? Every little step you take really will make a difference.

ADDRESSES AND WEB SITES

Find out more about what you can do to help save the planet by contacting some of the organizations listed below. You can write to them for more information, but remember to send a large stamped, self-addressed envelope.

Greenpeace
702 H Street NW
Washington, DC 20001
www.greenpeaceusa.org

World Wildlife Fund
1250 24th Street NW
P.O. Box 97180
Washington, DC 20037
www.worldwildlife.org

Friends of the Earth
1025 Vermont Ave NW
Washington, DC 20005
www.foe.org

Endangered Earth
A global source of
  information about the
  earth's endangered animals
www.endangeredearth.com

Recycle City
www.epa.gov/recyclecity/

The Nature Conservancy
Various addresses by state
http://nature.org/

Millennium Green
1-800-522-3557
http://www.green.gov/

Ozone Action
1700 Connecticut Ave NW
Suite 300
Washington, DC 20009
www.ozone.org

Surface Transportation
  Policy Project
1100 17th St. NW, 10th Fl.
Washington, DC 20036
http://www.transact.org

U.S. Environmental
  Protection Agency
1200 Pennsylvania Ave. NW
Washington, DC 20460
www.epa.gov/kids/

U.S. Fish and Wildlife
  Service
www.fws.gov